STRUM & SING

KELLY CLARKSON

ISBN 978-1-4950-2352-1

HAL•LEONARD®
CORPORATION

7777 W. BLUEMOUND RD. P.O. BOX 13819 MILWAUKEE, WI 53213

Visit Hal Leonard Online at
www.halleonard.com

Already Gone

Words and Music by
Kelly Clarkson and Ryan Tedder

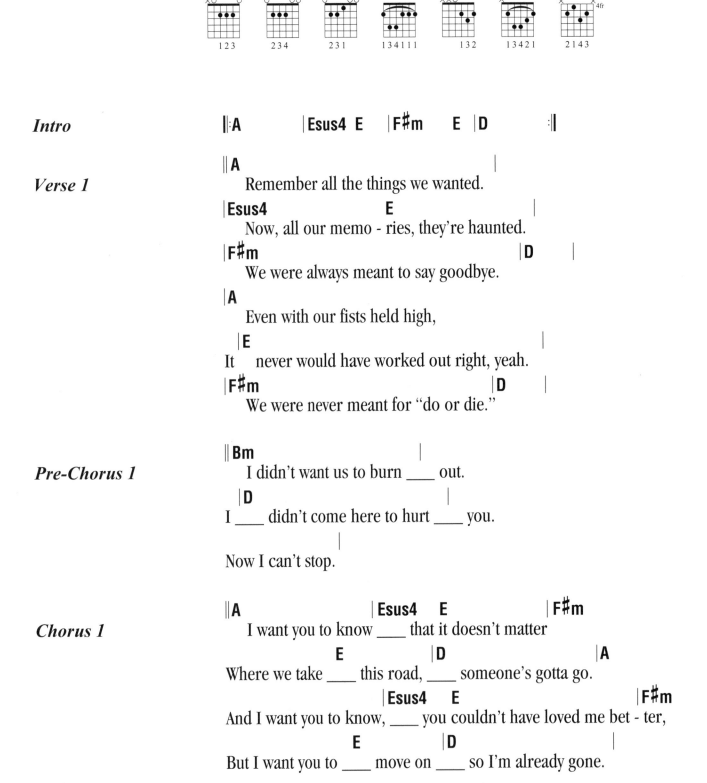

Intro   ‖: A |Esus4 E |F♯m   E |D   :‖

Verse 1   ‖A |
Remember all the things we wanted.
|Esus4   E |
Now, all our memo - ries, they're haunted.
|F♯m |D |
We were always meant to say goodbye.
|A
Even with our fists held high,
|E |
It   never would have worked out right, yeah.
|F♯m |D |
We were never meant for "do or die."

Pre-Chorus 1   ‖Bm |
I didn't want us to burn ___ out.
|D |
I ___ didn't come here to hurt ___ you.
|
Now I can't stop.

Chorus 1   ‖A |Esus4   E |F♯m
I want you to know ___ that it doesn't matter
E |D |A
Where we take ___ this road, ___ someone's gotta go.
|Esus4   E |F♯m
And I want you to know, ___ you couldn't have loved me bet - ter,
E |D |
But I want you to ___ move on ___ so I'm already gone.

Verse 2

```
‖A                              |
  Lookin' at you makes it harder,
|Esus4                E          |
  But I'll I know that you'll find another
|F♯m                            |D      |
  That doesn't always make you wanna cry.
|A
  It started with a perfect kiss,
   |Esus4           E          |
Then    we could feel the poison set in.
|F♯m                       |D      |
  Perfect couldn't keep this love alive.
```

Pre-Chorus 2

```
‖B                   |
  You know that I love ____ you so.
  |D              |            |
I ____ love you enough ____ to let you go.
```

Chorus 2

```
‖A                  |Esus4   E        |F♯m
  I want you to know ____ that it doesn't matter
            E          |D              |A
Where we take ____ this road, ____ someone's gotta go.
                   |Esus4      E           |F♯m
And I want you to know, ____ you couldn't have loved me bet - ter,
           E          |D              |A
But I want you to ____ move on ____ so I'm already gone.
                 |E              |F♯m
I'm already gone. ____ I'm already gone.
           E          |D                        |A
You can't make it feel right ____ when you know that it's wrong.
                 |E              |F♯m
I'm already gone, ____ already gone.
           E          |D                  |
There's no movin' on, ____ so I'm already gone.
```

Bridge

```
‖A                      |E              |F♯m                |D        |
```
(Gone, already gone, ___ already gone, ___ already gone.
```
|A                      |E              |F♯m                |D        |
```
 Gone, already gone, ___ already gone, ___ already gone.)

Verse 3

```
‖A                                     |
```
    Remember all the things we wanted.
```
|E                                     |
```
    Now all our memories, they're haunted.
```
|F♯m                     E            |D      |
```
    We were always meant to say goodbye.

Chorus 3

```
‖A                 |Esus4    E              |F♯m
```
    I want you to know ___ that it doesn't matter
```
                  E          |D                    |A
```
Where we take ___ this road, ___ someone's gotta go.
```
                        |Esus4    E                    |F♯m
```
And I want you to know, ___ you couldn't have loved me bet - ter,
```
                        E          |D                    |A
```
But I want you to ___ move on ___ so I'm already gone.
```
                    |E            |F♯m
```
I'm already gone. ___ I'm already gone.
```
              E        |D                          |A
```
You can't make it feel right ___ when you know that it's wrong.
```
                    |E              |F♯m
```
I'm already gone, ___ already gone.
```
              E        |D                    |Dmaj9      ‖
```
There's no movin' on, ___ so I'm already gone.

Breakaway

from THE PRINCESS DIARIES 2: ROYAL ENGAGEMENT

Words and Music by Bridget Benenate,
Avril Lavigne and Matthew Gerrard

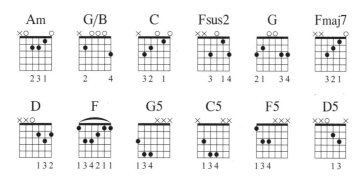

Intro

```
||Am           G/B         |
  Dah, dah, dah, dah, dah.
|C            Fsus2        |
  Dah, dah, dah, dah, dah.
|Am           G/B          |Fsus2   |
  Dah, dah, dah, dah, dah, dah, dah.
|Am           G/B          |
  Dah, dah, dah, dah, dah.
|C            Fsus2        |
  Dah, dah, dah, dah, dah.
|Am           G           |Fsus2   |
  Dah, dah, dah, dah, dah, dah, dah.
```

Verse 1

```
||Am           G/B          |
  Grew up in a small town
|C                   Fsus2        |
  And when the rain would fall down,
|Am      G/B   |Fsus2   |
  I'd just stare out my window,
|Am            G/B          |
  Dreamin' of what could be
|C                Fsus2   |
  And if I'd end up happy.
|Am   G   |Fsus2        |
  I      would pray.
```

Verse 2

```
‖ Am            G/B         |
   Tryin' hard to reach out
| C                Fsus2     |
   But when I tried to speak out
| Am      G/B        | Fsus2  |
   Felt like no one could hear me.
| Am            G/B          |
   Wanted to be - long here
| C                   Fsus2          |
   But something felt so wrong here.
| Am   G | Fsus2
  So   I'd  pray
           | Am      G | D   | F   G   |
I could break a - way.
```

Chorus 1

```
‖ C                        | G
   I'll spread my wings and I'll learn how to fly.
  | Am             | Fsus2
I'll do what it takes till I touch the sky.
    | C                            |
I'll    make a wish, take a chance,
| G                   | Am     G | Fsus2    |
   Make a change and break - a - way.
| C                    | G
 Out of the darkness and into the sun,
   | Am                  | Fsus2
But I won't forget all the ones ____ that I love.
   | C                          |
I'll    take a risk, take a chance,
| G                 | Am     G | Fsus2    |
   Make a change and break - a - way.
```

Interlude

```
‖ Am            G/B         |
   Dah, dah, dah, dah, dah.
| C            Fsus2        |
   Dah, dah, dah, dah, dah.
| Am           G           | Fsus2     |
   Dah, dah, dah, dah, dah, dah, dah.
```

Verse 3

```
||Am          G/B      |
   Wanna feel the warm breeze,
|C          Fsus2       |
   Sleep under a palm tree,
|Am       G/B    |Fsus2   |
   Feel the rush of the ocean,
|Am          G/B         |
   Get on board a fast train,
|C          Fsus2        |
   Travel on a jet plane
|Am   G |Fsus2
 Far    a - way
     |Am     G |D   |F    G   |
And break - a - way.
```

Chorus 2

Repeat Chorus 1

Bridge

```
|| G5                          |
   Buildings with a hundred floors.
|C5                F5              |
   Swingin' 'round re - volving doors.
|G5                          |C5   F5
   Maybe I don't know where they'll take me.
      |G5              |C5
But     gotta keep movin' on, movin' on,
F5      |D5          |F5    G5    |
   Fly a - way, break a - way.
```

Chorus 3

```
|| C                      |G          |
   I'll spread my wings and I'll learn how to fly.
|Am                 |Fsus2
 Though it's not easy to tell ____ you goodbye,
      |C                        |
Gotta    take a risk, take a chance,
|G                 |Am    G |Fsus2   |
   Make a change and break - a - way.
|C                 |G
 Out of the darkness and into the sun,
   |Am              |Fsus2
But I won't forget the place I come from.
      |C                        |
I gotta    take a risk, take a chance,
|G                 |Am    G |Fsus2   |
   Make a change and break - a - way,
|Am    G |Fsus2 |Am    G |Fsus2    ||
 Break - a - way,    break - a - way.
```

Because of You

Words and Music by
Kelly Clarkson, David Hodges
and Ben Moody

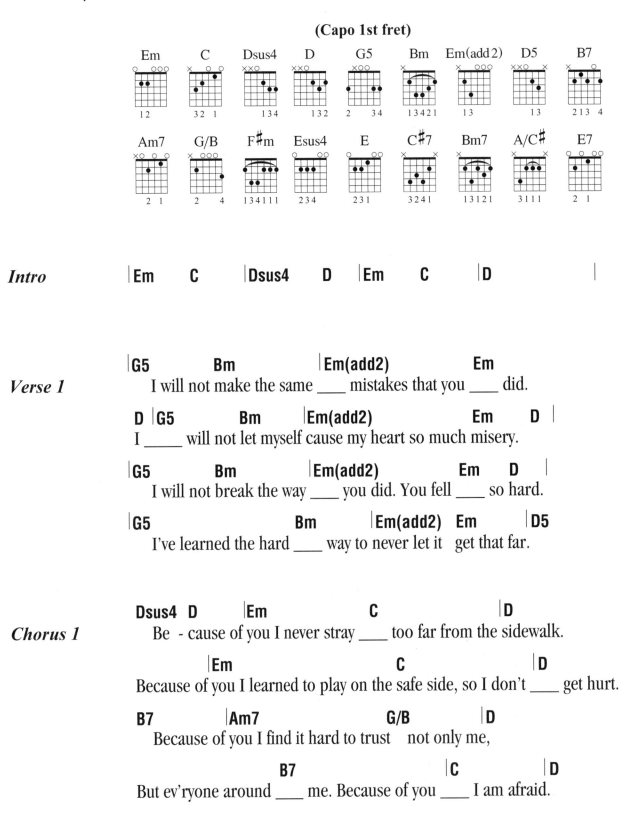

(Capo 1st fret)

Intro | Em   C | Dsus4   D | Em   C | D | |

Verse 1

| G5   Bm | Em(add2)   Em
I will not make the same ___ mistakes that you ___ did.

D | G5   Bm | Em(add2)   Em   D |
I ____ will not let myself cause my heart so much misery.

| G5   Bm | Em(add2)   Em   D |
I will not break the way ___ you did. You fell ___ so hard.

| G5   Bm | Em(add2) Em | D5
I've learned the hard ___ way to never let it get that far.

Chorus 1

Dsus4 D | Em   C | D
Be - cause of you I never stray ___ too far from the sidewalk.

| Em   C | D
Because of you I learned to play on the safe side, so I don't ___ get hurt.

B7 | Am7   G/B | D
Because of you I find it hard to trust   not only me,

B7 | C | D
But ev'ryone around ___ me. Because of you ___ I am afraid.

Verse 2

|G5   Bm |Em(add2)   Em   D |G5

I lose my way, and it's not too long before ____ you point it out.

Bm |Em(add2)   Em   D |G5

I cannot cry, be - cause I know that's weakness in ____ your eyes.

Bm |Em(add2)   Em   D |G5

I'm forced to fake a smile, ____ a laugh, ev - 'ry day ____ of my life.

Bm |Em(add2) Em |D5

My heart can't possibly break when it wasn't even whole to start ___ with.

Chorus 2   *Repeat Chorus 1*

Bridge

|D |Bm   Em |Dsus4   D

I watched you die, I heard you cry ev'ry night in your ___ sleep.

|Bm   Em |Dsus4

I was so young, you should have known better than to lean ___ on me.

|Bm   Em |Dsus4

You never thought of anyone else, you just saw your pain,

D |Bm   Em |Dsus4   D |Dsus4   D

And now I cry in the middle of the night for the same damn thing.

Chorus 3

Dsus4 D |Em   C |D

Be - cause of you I never stray ___ too far from the sidewalk.

|Em   C |D

Because of you I learned to play on the safe side, so I don't ___ get hurt.

N.C. |F#m   D |Esus4   E

Because of you I try my hardest just ___ to forget ev - 'rything.

Esus4 E |F#m   D |E

Be - cause of you, I don't know how to let anyone else ___ in.

C#7 |Bm7   A/C# |E7

Because of you ___ I'm ashamed of my life, because it's emp - ty.

C#7 |D |E | F#m D|

Because of you ___ I am afraid, ___ because of you,

|E Esus4 E |F#m D |E ‖

Be - cause of you.

Behind These Hazel Eyes

Words and Music by Kelly Clarkson,
Lukasz Gottwald and Max Martin

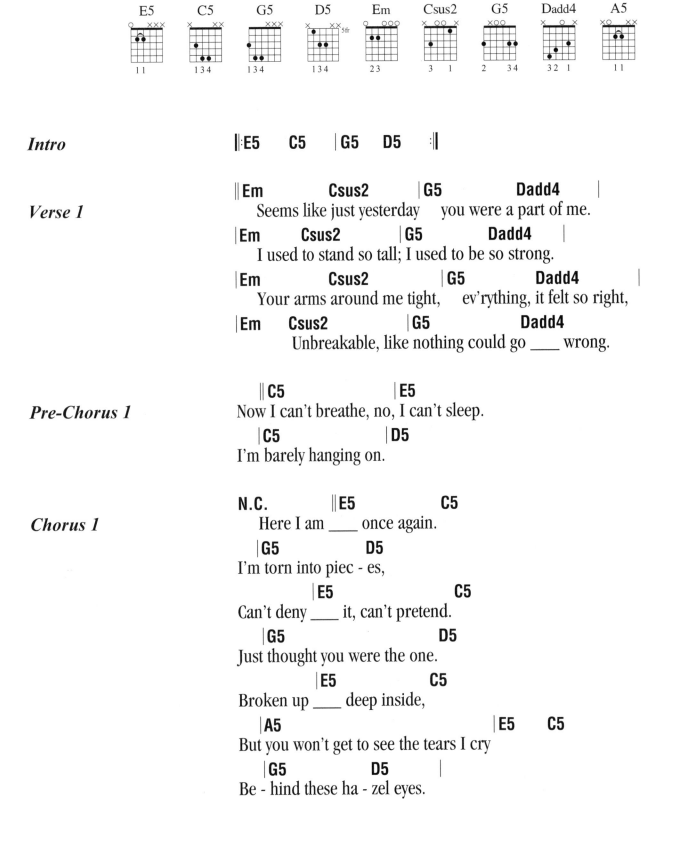

(Capo 2nd fret)

E5   C5   G5   D5   Em   Csus2   G5   Dadd4   A5

Intro

‖: E5   C5 | G5   D5   :‖

Verse 1

‖ Em   Csus2 | G5   Dadd4 |
  Seems like just yesterday   you were a part of me.
| Em   Csus2 | G5   Dadd4 |
  I used to stand so tall; I used to be so strong.
| Em   Csus2 | G5   Dadd4 |
  Your arms around me tight,   ev'rything, it felt so right,
| Em   Csus2 | G5   Dadd4 |
  Unbreakable, like nothing could go ___ wrong.

Pre-Chorus 1

‖ C5 | E5 |
Now I can't breathe, no, I can't sleep.
| C5 | D5 |
I'm barely hanging on.

Chorus 1

N.C.   ‖ E5   C5 |
  Here I am ___ once again.
| G5   D5 |
I'm torn into piec - es,
            | E5   C5 |
Can't deny ___ it, can't pretend.
| G5   D5 |
Just thought you were the one.
            | E5   C5 |
Broken up ___ deep inside,
| A5 | E5   C5 |
But you won't get to see the tears I cry
| G5   D5 |
Be - hind these ha - zel eyes.

Verse 2

```
‖Em     Csus2     |G5          Dadd4        |
  I told you ev'rything,     opened up and let you in.
|Em        Csus2              |G5       Dadd4        |
   You made me feel all right for once in my ___ life.
|Em        Csus2        |G5          Dadd4         |
   Now all that's left of me     is what I pretend to be;
|Em  Csus2              |G5           Dadd4       |
So ___ together, but so broken up in - side,
```

Pre-Chorus 2

```
      ‖C5              |E5
  'Cause I can't breathe, no, I can't sleep.
      |C5             |D5
I'm barely hanging on.
```

Chorus 2

Repeat Chorus 1

Bridge

```
‖A5     N.C.        |G5
  Swallow me then spit me out.
   |A5    N.C.       |E5         |
For hating you I blame my - self.
|A5      N.C.                 |G5
  Seeing you, it kills me now.
              |A5           |C5     D5        |Em    Csus2    |
No, I don't ___ cry on the out - side ___ anymore,
|G5   Dadd4      |Em    Csus2   |D5
            Anymore.
```

Chorus 3

Repeat Chorus 1

Outro-Chorus

Repeat Chorus 1

Catch My Breath

Words and Music by
Kelly Clarkson, Jason Halbert
and Eric Olson

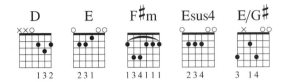

Intro | |D | |E   F#m |D | |E   F#m | |

| |D | |E   F#m |E | | | |

Verse 1

| |D |
I don't wanna be left ___ behind.

|E   F#m |D |
Dis - tance was a friend ___ of mine.

|F#m   E |D |
Catch - ing breath in a web ___ of lies.

|E F#m |Esus4 |E
I've spent most of my life

|D |
Riding waves playing ac - robat,

|E   F#m |D |
Shad - owboxing the oth - er half,

|F#m   E |D |
Learn - ing how to ___ react.

|E F#m |Esus4 |E
I've spent most of my time…

Pre-Chorus 1

         |D |E
Catching my breath, letting it go,

        |F#m |E/G#
Turning my cheek for the sake of the show.

        |D |E
Now that you know, this is my life,

      |F#m |E/G# |
I won't be told what's supposed to be right.

Chorus 1

|D |E |
Catch my breath,   no one can hold me back.

|D |E |
   I ain't got time for that.

|D |E |
Catch my breath,   won't let 'em get me down.

|D |E |
   It's all so simple now.

Verse 2

| |D |
 Addicted to the love ____ I found,

|E   F#m |D |
  Heavy heart, now a weight - less cloud.

|F#m   E |D |
  Mak - ing time for the ones ____ that count,

|E F#m |Esus4 |E
I'll spend the rest of my time

            |D |
Laughing hard with the win - dows down

|E   F#m |D |
  Leav - ing footprints all o - ver town.

|F#m   E |D |
  Keep - ing faith, karma comes ____ around.

|E F#m |Esus4 |E
I will spend the rest of my life…

Pre-Chorus 2   *Repeat Pre-Chorus 1*

Chorus 2   *Repeat Chorus 1*

Bridge

```
|D  |E      F#m  |D        |
You helped me see
```
```
|E  F#m     |D  |E F#m  |Esus4      |
The beau - ty        in ev'rything.
```

Pre-Chorus 3

```
|N.C.          |D              |E
Catching my breath, letting it go,
```
```
F#m           |D                    |F#m
  Turning my cheek for the sake of the show.
```
```
E          |D             |E
  Now that you know, this is my life,
```
```
F#m         |Esus4                  |E
  I won't be told what's supposed to be right.
```

Pre-Chorus 4   *Repeat Pre-Chorus 1*

Chorus 3

```
|D            |E                          |
Catch my breath,    no one can hold me back.
```
```
|D                     |E        |
  I ain't got time for that.
```
```
|D            |E                          |
Catch my breath,    won't let 'em get me down.
```
```
|D                    |E                  |
  It's all so simple now. ____ It's all so simple now.
```

Pre-Chorus 5   *Repeat Pre-Chorus 1*

Chorus 4   *Repeat Chorus 1*

Outro

```
|D              |E        F#m  |D            |
|E              |              |            ‖
```

Heartbeat Song

Words and Music by Jason Evigan,
Mitch Allan, Kara DioGuardi and Audra Mae

Tune down 1/2 step:
(low to high) E♭-A♭-D♭-G♭-B♭-E♭

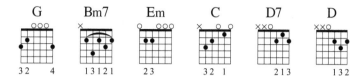

Chorus 1

    N.C.   **‖G** |
This is my heart - beat song and I'm ___ gonna play it.
    |Bm7 | **|Em**
Been ___ so long, I forgot ___ how to turn it up, ___ up, up, up
    | **|C** | **|N.C.** |
All ___ night long, oh, up, ___ up all night long.

Verse 1

    ‖G | |
 You, where the hell did you come from?
|Bm7 | **|Em**
 You're a diff'rent, diff'rent kind of fun,
   | **|C** | |
And I'm so used to feelin' numb.

Verse 2

    ‖G | |
 Now I've got pins and needles on my tongue,
|Bm7 | |
 An - ticipatin' what's to come,
|Em | **|C** | |
 Like a finger on a loaded gun.

Pre-Chorus 1

    ‖G | **|Bm7** | |
 I can feel ___ it rising temper'ture ___ inside me.
|Em | **|D7** |
Haven't felt ___ it for a long ___ time.

Chorus 2

| N.C.   ‖**G** |

   This is my heart - beat song and I'm ___ gonna play it.

   |**Bm7** | |**Em**

Been ___ so long, I forgot ___ how to turn it up, ___ up, up, up

   | |**C** |

All ___ night long, oh, up, ___ up all night long.

| |**G** |

   This is my heart - beat song and I'm ___ gonna play it.

   |**Bm7** | |**Em**

Turned ___ it on, but I know ___ you can take it up, ___ up, up, up

   | |**C** | |

All ___ night long, oh, up, ___ up all night, all ___ night long.

Verse 3

‖**G** | |**Bm7**

   I, I wasn't even gonna go out.

   | |**Em**

But I never would have had a doubt

   | |**C** | |

If I'd a known where I'd be now.

Pre-Chorus 2

‖**G** | |**Bm7** |

   Your hands on ___ my hips and my kiss on ___ your lips,

|**Em** | |**D7** |

Oh, I could do ___ this for a long ___ time.

Chorus 3

| N.C.   ‖**G** |

   This is my heart - beat song and I'm ___ gonna play it.

   |**Bm7** | |**Em**

Been ___ so long, I forgot ___ how to turn it up, ___ up, up, up

   | |**C** |

All ___ night long, oh, up, ___ up all night long.

| |**G** |

   This is my heart - beat song and I'm ___ gonna play it.

   |**Bm7** | |**Em**

Turned ___ it on, but I know ___ you can take it up, ___ up, up, up

   | |**C** |

All ___ night long, oh, up, ___ up all night long.

Bridge

```
|                          ‖D                   |
        Until tonight I only dreamed about you.
|                        |Em                |
        I can't believe I ever breathed without you.
|              D         |C            |
        Baby, you make me feel a - live and brand new.
|              |         |         |
Bring it one more time.
```

Chorus 4

```
|                        ‖G              |
        This is my heart - beat song and I'm ____ gonna play it.
    |Bm7                 |              |Em
Been ____ so long, I forgot ____ how to turn it up, ____ up, up, up
        |                   |C
All ____ night long, oh, up, ____ up all night long.
|                |G              |
        This is my heart - beat song and I'm ____ gonna play it.
        |Bm7              |            |Em
Turned ____ it on, but I know ____ you can take it up, ____ up, up, up
        |                 |C           |
All ____ night long, oh, up, ____ up all night long.
|                |G              |
        This is my heart - beat song and I'm ____ gonna play it.
    |Bm7              |            |Em
Been ____ so long, I forgot ____ how to turn it up, ____ up, up, up
        |                 |C           |
All ____ night long, oh, up, ____ up all night long.
|                |N.C.           |
        This is my heart - beat song and I'm ____ gonna play it.
        |              |            |
Turned ____ it on, but I know ____ you can take it up,
|              |              |              ‖
        Up, up, up all ____ night long, oh, up, ____ up all night long.
```

Dark Side

Words and Music by
busbee and Alex Geringas

Intro

‖D | | |G5 | Gm6 |

Oh, oh,

|D | |Gm6 |

Oh, oh, ___ oh, oh.

Verse 1

‖D | |Gm6/D |

There's a place _____ that I know.

| |D | |Gm6/B♭ |

It's not pret - ty there and few ___ have ever gone.

| |Bm | |Gm |

If I show it to you now will it make you run away?

Verse 2

| ‖D | |Gm6 |

Or will you stay ___ even if it hurts?

| |D | |Gm6 |

Even if I try to push you out ___ will you return

| |Bm |

And remind me who I really am?

| |Gm | |

Please remind me who I really am.

Chorus 1

‖Bm |D |

Ev'rybody's got a dark ___ side.

|G |Em |

Do you love ___ me? Can you love ___ mine?

|Bm |D |G

Nobody's a picture per - fect, but we're worth ___ it.

|Em

You know that we're worth ___ it.

|Bm | |Gm |

Will you love ___ me ___ even with my dark side?

Verse 3

| ‖**D** | |**Gm6** |
Like a dia - mond ___ from black dust,

| |**D** | |**Gm6** |
It's hard to know ___ what can become ___ if you give up.

| |**Bm** |
So don't give up ___ on me.

| |**Gm** | |
Please remind me who I really am.

Chorus 2   *Repeat Chorus 1*

Bridge

| ‖**D** | |**G**
       Don't run away. ___ Don't run away.

| |**Bm** |
Just tell me that you will stay.

| |**G** | |
Promise me you will stay. ___ Yeah, ___ yeah.

|**D** | |**G**
   Don't run away. ___ Don't run away.

| |**Bm** |
Just promise me you will stay.

| |**G** |
Promise me you will stay.

| |**Bm** | |**Gm** | |
   Will you love ___ me?   Ooh.

Chorus 3   *Repeat Chorus 1*

Outro

| ‖**D** | |**Gm** | |
      Don't run away. ___ Don't run away.

|**D** | | **Gm**| ‖
Don't run away. ___ Promise you'll   stay.

Invincible

Words and Music by Warren Felder,
Steve Mostyn, Sia Furler and Jesse Shatkin

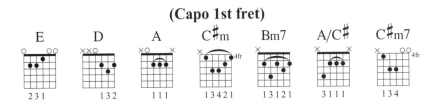

(Capo 1st fret)

E   D   A   C#m   Bm7   A/C#   C#m7

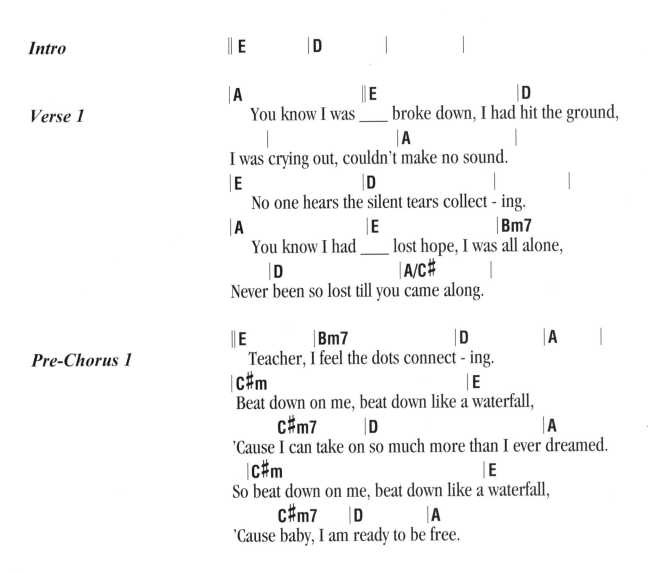

Intro

‖E |D | |

Verse 1

|A   ‖E |D
You know I was ___ broke down, I had hit the ground,

| |A |
I was crying out, couldn't make no sound.

|E |D | |
No one hears the silent tears collect - ing.

|A |E |Bm7
You know I had ___ lost hope, I was all alone,

|D |A/C# |
Never been so lost till you came along.

Pre-Chorus 1

‖E |Bm7 |D |A |
Teacher, I feel the dots connect - ing.

|C#m |E
Beat down on me, beat down like a waterfall,

|C#m7 |D |A
'Cause I can take on so much more than I ever dreamed.

|C#m |E
So beat down on me, beat down like a waterfall,

|C#m7 |D |A
'Cause baby, I am ready to be free.

Chorus 1

```
           ‖E      |Bm7
Now I am in - vinci - ble,
               |D                    |A/C♯
No, I ain't a scared little girl no more.
               |E      |Bm7                    |
Yeah, I am in - vinci - ble, what was I running for?
|D        |A
(Oh, woh, woh.)
               |E        |Bm7
I was hiding from the world,
               |D              |A/C♯
I was so a - fraid I felt so un - sure.
               |E      |Bm7
Now I am in - vinci - ble,
                        |D            |A
Another perfect storm. ___ (Oh, woh, woh.)
```

Verse 2

```
           ‖E          |D
Now I am a   warrior, a shooting star,
           |                |A            |
Know I got this far, had a broken heart.
|E                  |D          |        |
    No one hears the silent tears collect - ing.
|A                |E                    |Bm7
  'Cause it's being   weak but strong in the truth I found,
        |D              |A/C♯          |
I have courage now, gonna shout it out.
```

Pre-Chorus 2   *Repeat Pre-Chorus 1*

Chorus 2   *Repeat Chorus 1*

Bridge

```
‖E            |D              |        |C♯m7       |
  I was running from an empty threat of emptiness.
|E            |D              |        |C♯m7       |
  I was running from an empty threat that didn't exist.
|E            |D              |        |C♯m7       |
  I was running from an empty threat of a - bandonment.
|E            |D              |        |C♯m7      E |    |    |
  I was running from an empty threat, that didn't exist, oh.
```

Chorus 3

```
|                    |E    |Bm7
    But now I am in - vinci - ble,
              |D              |C♯m
No, I ain't a scared little girl no more.
              |E    |Bm7                |    |
Yeah, I am in - vinci - ble, what was I running for?
|            |E    |Bm7            |D            |A/C♯
  I was hiding from the world, I was so a - fraid I felt so un - sure.
              |E    |Bm7                    |D        |
Now I am in - vinci - ble, another perfect storm. ___ (Oh, woh,
|A              |E    |Bm7          |D              |A/C♯
 Woh.) Now I am in - vinci - ble, no I ain't a scared little girl no more.
              |E    |Bm7                |
Yeah, I am in - vinci - ble, what was I running for?
|D                              |
   (What was I running for?)
|A            |E    |Bm7
  I was hiding from the world,
              |D            |A/C♯
I was so a - fraid, I was so un - sure.
              |E    |Bm7                  |D        |A    ‖
Now I am in - vinci - ble, another perfect storm. ___ (Oh, woh.)
```

Mr. Know It All

Words and Music by Esther Dean,
Brian Seals, Brett James and Dante Jones

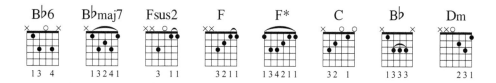

Intro   ‖Bb6 Bbmaj7 |Bb6 Bbmaj7 |Fsus2 F |Fsus2 F |

Verse 1

‖F* |
    Mister Know It All, well, you,   you think you know it all,
       |C
But you   don't know a thing at all.
      |
Ain't it,   ain't it something y'all,
      |Bb |
When somebody tells you something 'bout you,
|
Think that they know you more than you do.
     |F* | |
So you   take it down, another pill to swallow.

Verse 2

‖F* |
    Mister Bring Me Down, well, you,
| |
   You like to bring me down, don't you?
|C |
   But I ain't layin' down, baby,   I ain't goin' down.
   |Bb |
Can't nobody tell me how it's gonna be,
|
Nobody gonna make a fool out of me.
   |F* |
Baby,   you should know that I lead, not follow.

Chorus 1

       | ‖**F*** |

Oh, you think that you know ___ me, know me,

    | |**C** |

That's why I'm leaving you lone - ly, lonely.

    | |**B♭** |

'Cause, baby, you don't know a thing about me.

    | |**F*** | |

You don't know a thing about me.

    | |

You ain't got the right to tell me

| |

When and where to go, no right to tell me.

|**C** |

Acting like you own me, lately.

    | |**B♭** |

Yeah, baby, you don't know a thing about me,

    | |**F*** | |

You don't know a thing about me.

Verse 3

‖**F*** |

Mister Play Your Games, only   got yourself to blame

      |**C** |

When you   want me back again but I   ain't falling back again.

      |**B♭** |

'Cause I'm living my truth without your lies.

| |

Let's be clear, baby, this is goodbye.

|**F*** |

I ain't coming back tomorrow.

Chorus 2

Repeat Chorus 1

Bridge

`‖Dm` `|C`
So what, you've got the world at your feet
`|B♭` `|` `|`
And you know ev'rything about ev'rything, but you don't.
`|Dm` `|C` `|B♭` `|`
You still think I'm coming back, but baby, you'll see ___ yeah.

Chorus 3

`|` `‖F*` `|`
Oh, you think that you know ___ me, know me,
`|` `|C` `|`
That's why I'm leaving you lone - ly, lonely.
`|` `|B♭` `|`
'Cause, baby, you don't know a thing about me.
`|` `|F*` `|` `|`
You don't know a thing about me.
`|` `|`
You ain't got the right to tell me
`|` `|`
When and where to go, no right to tell me.
`|C` `|`
Acting like you own me, lately.
`|` `|B♭` `|`
Yeah, baby, you don't know a thing about me,
`|` `|F*` `|` `|`
You don't know a thing about me.

Outro

`‖` `|`
Mister Know It All, well, you, you think you know it all,
`|C`
But you don't know a thing at all.
`|` `|B♭` `|`
And you, yeah, baby, you don't know a thing about me,
`|` `|F*` `|` `‖`
You don't know a thing about me.

Miss Independent

Words and Music by Kelly Clarkson, Christina Aguilera,
Rhett Lawrence and Matthew Morris

B9   E9   B5   D5   E5   G5   A5   E/G#

Bm   G   D   F#7   D/A   F#7/A#   F#7/C#

Intro

‖ B9 | | | |

Verse 1

‖ B9 | |
    Miss Independent. ___ Miss Self Sufficient.

| | | |
    Miss Keep Your Distance. ___   Miss Unafraid.

| | | |
    Miss Out Of My Way.   Miss Don't Let A Man In - terfere, no.

| E9 |
    Miss On Her Own. ___ Miss Almost Grown.

| B9 |
Miss Never Let A Man Help ___ Her Off Her Throne.

| E9 | |
So by keepin' her heart protected she'd never, ever feel rejected.

| | N.C. |
Little Miss Apprehensive. Said, ooh, she fell in love.

Chorus 1

‖ B5   D5 |
    What is this feelin' tak - in' over?

| E5   G5   A5 |
Thinkin' no one could o - pen the door.

| B5   D5 | G5   E/G#   A5 |
    Surprise,   it's time   to feel   what's real.

| B5   D5 |
What happened to Miss In - dependent?

| E5   G5   A5 |
No longer needs to be ___ defens - ive.

| B5   D5 | G5   E/G#   A5 |
    Goodbye   on you.   Real love   is true.

Interlude

| B9 | |

Verse 2

```
‖B9                    |
```
Miss Guided Heart. Miss Play It Smart.
```
        |                      |            |
```
Miss If You Wanna Use That Line You Better Not Start, no.
```
    |                |                   |
```
But she miscalculated. She didn't wanna end up jaded
```
    |                              |
```
And this Miss decided not to miss ___ out on true love.
```
        |E9                        |
```
So by changin' the misconceptions she went in a new direction
```
    |                          |N.C.              |
```
And found inside she felt a connection.   She fell in love.

Chorus 2

Repeat Chorus 1

Bridge

```
‖Bm                |              |
```
When Miss Independ - ent walked away,
```
|G                |            |
```
No time for a love ___ that came her way.
```
|D              |              |
```
She looked in the mir - ror and thought today,
```
|F♯7            |          |
```
What happened to Miss   No Longer Afraid?
```
|Bm             |            |
```
It took some time ___ for her to see
```
|G                    |           |
```
How beautiful love ___ could truly be.
```
|D/A            |          |
```
No more talk of what   cannot be real.
```
|F♯7/A♯        |F♯7/C♯        |
```
I'm so glad I fi - n'lly feel.

Chorus 3

```
‖ B5              D5        |
```
What is this feelin' tak - in' over?
```
|E5              G5      A5    |
```
Thinkin' no one could o - pen the door.
```
|B5        D5    |G5    E/G♯        A5  |
```
Surprise,   it's time   to feel   what's real.
```
|B5                      D5        |
```
What happened to Miss In - dependent?
```
|E5              G5        A5    |
```
No longer needs to be ___ defens - ive.
```
|B5        D5    |G5      E/G♯      A5    |
```
Goodbye   on you.   Real love,   real love ___ is true.

Outro

```
| B9      |          |              |      ‖
```
Miss Independent.

A Moment Like This

Words and Music by
John Reid and Jorgen Kjell Elofsson

(Capo 1st fret)

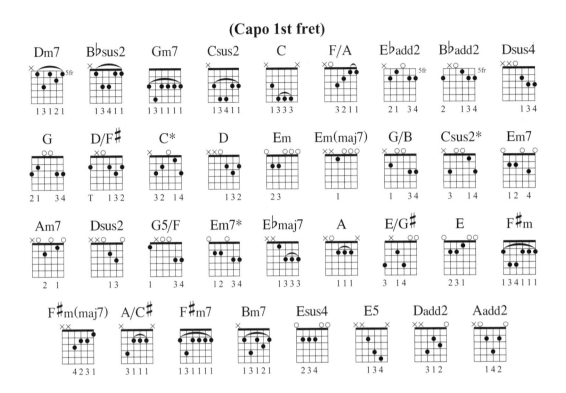

Intro

|| Dm7 B♭sus2 | Gm7 Csus2 |

Verse 1

|| Dm7   B♭sus2 | Gm7   Csus2 |
    What if I told ___ you it was all meant to be?

| Dm7   B♭sus2 | Gm7   C |
    Would you be - lieve me?   Would you agree?

| Dm7   B♭sus2 | F/A   Gm7 |
    It's almost that feeling   we've met before,

| E♭add2 | B♭add2 |
So tell me that you don't think I'm cra - zy

| Gm7 | C |
When I tell you love has come here and now.

Chorus 1

    Dsus4

A moment like this.

‖**G**   **D/F♯** |**C***   **D**

   Some people wait a life - time for a moment like this.

|**G**   **D/F♯** |**C***   **D**

   Some people search for - ever for that one special kiss.

|**Em**   **Em(maj7)** |**G**   **G/B**   **Csus2***

   Oh, I can't believe it's hap - pening ____ to me.

   |**Em7**   **Am7** |**Dsus2** |**G**

Some people wait a life - time for a moment like this.

Verse 2

   ‖ **Dm7**   **B♭sus2** |**Gm7**   **C**

    Ev'rything changes, but beauty remains

|**Dm7**   **B♭sus2** |**Gm7**   **C**

  Something so tender   I can't explain.

|**Dm7**   **B♭sus2** |**F/A**   **Gm7**

   Well, I may be dreaming, but still lie awake.

|**E♭add2** |**B♭add2**

 Can't we make this dream last forever?

    |**Gm7** |**C**

And I'll cherish all the love we share.

Chorus 2

    Dsus4

A moment like this.

‖**G**   **D/F♯** |**C***   **D**

   Some people wait a life - time for a moment like this.

|**G**   **D/F♯** |**C***   **D**

   Some people search for - ever for that one special kiss.

|**Em**   **Em(maj7)** |**G**   **G/B**   **Csus2***

   Oh, I can't believe it's hap - pening ____ to me.

   |**Em7**   **Am7** |**D**

Some people wait a life - time for a moment like this.

Bridge

```
‖G  G5/F      |Em7*              E♭maj7    |G
         Could ___ this be the great - est love of all?
    G5/F      |Em7*              E♭maj7              |
      I wanna know that you will catch ___ me when I fall,
    |Em  Em(maj7)    |G    G/B   Csus2* |
              So let me tell you this…
       |Em7          Am7        |Dsus2              |
    Some people wait a life - time for a moment like this.
```

Chorus 3

```
    ‖A  E/G♯                |D        E             |
         Some people wait a life - time for a moment like this.
    |A       E/G♯          |D         E             |
       Some people search for - ever for that one special kiss.
    |F♯m   F♯m(maj7)          |A        A/C♯   D
       Oh, I can't believe it's hap - pening ___ to me.
       |F♯m          Bm7        |E              |
    Some people wait a life - time for a moment like this.
    |A   E/G♯  |D    Esus4  E  |A   E/G♯  |D   Esus4   E
                Oh, moment like this.          (Moment like.)
       |F♯m  F♯m(maj7)      |A       A/C♯        D   |
    Oh, ___ I can't believe it's hap - pening ___ to me.
       |F♯m7          Bm7        |E5             |A  E/G♯
    Some people wait a life - time for a moment like this.
    |Dadd2  E          |Aadd2   ‖
       Oh, ___ like this.
```

People Like Us

Words and Music by James Michael,
Meghan Kabir and Blair Daly

Tune down 1/2 step:
(low to high) Eb-Ab-Db-Gb-Bb-Eb

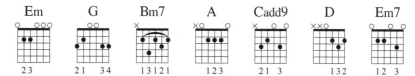

Intro

‖**Em** | | |
Spoken: We come into this world unknown.
|**G** | |**Bm7** |
But know that we are not alone.
| |**A** |
They try and knock us down.   A change is coming,
| | |
And it's our time now.

Verse 1

‖**Em** | |**G** |
Hey,   ev'rybody loses it.
| |**Bm7** | |**A** |
Ev'rybody wants to throw it all away some - times.
| |**Em7** | |**G** |
And hey,   yeah, I know what you're going through.
| |**Bm7** | |**A** |
Don't let it get the best of you; you'll make it out a - live.

Pre-Chorus 1

| ‖**Cadd9** |**G** |
Oh, people like us, we've got to stick together.
|**D** |**Em7**   **Bm7** |
Keep your head up, nothing lasts forev - er.
|**Cadd9** |**G** |
Here's to the damned, to the lost and forgotten.
|**D** |**N.C.** |
It's hard to get high when you're living on the bottom.

Chorus 1

‖C |G
(Oh, whoa, oh, whoa.)

        |D |Em7 |
We are all misfits living in a world on fire.

|C |G
(Oh, whoa, oh, whoa.)

         |D |Em7 |
Sing it for the people like us, the people like us.

Verse 2

‖Em | |G |
  Hey,   well this is not a funeral.

| |Bm7 | |A |
    It's a revolution after all your tears have turned to rage.

| |Em7 | |G |
Just wait,   ev'rything will be okay,

| |Bm7 | |A |
   Even when you're feeling like it's going down in flames.

Pre-Chorus 2   *Repeat Pre-Chorus 1*

Chorus 2

‖C |G
(Oh, whoa, oh, whoa.)

        |D |Em7 |
We are all misfits living in a world on fire.

|C |G
(Oh, whoa, oh, whoa.)

         |D |Em7 |
Sing it for the people like us, the people like us.

|C |G
(Oh, whoa, oh, whoa.)

        |D |Em7 |
You've just got to turn it up loud when the flames get higher.

|C |G
(Oh, whoa, oh, whoa.)

        |D |Em7 |
Sing it for the people like us, the people like us.

Bridge

```
‖Cadd9                        |G                              |
```
They can't do nothing to you,   they can't do nothing to me.
```
|D                            |Em7                            |
```
This is the life that we choose,   this is the life that we bleed.
```
|Cadd9                        |G                                |
```
So throw your fists in the air,   come out, come out if you dare.
```
|D                            |Em7            |
```
Tonight we're gonna change ____ forever.
```
|Em          |            |G            |
```
            Ev'rybody loses it.
```
|            |Bm7              |            |A          |
```
Ev'rybody wants to throw it all away some - times.

Pre-Chorus 3   *Repeat Pre-Chorus 1*

Chorus 3   *Repeat Chorus 2*

Chorus 4
```
‖C            |G            |
```
(Oh, whoa, oh, whoa.)
```
              |D                |Em7            |
```
We are all misfits living in a world on fire.
```
|C            |G            |
```
(Oh, whoa, oh, whoa.)
```
                |D              |Em7              |
```
Sing it for the people like us, the people like us.
```
|C            |G            |
```
(Oh, whoa, oh, whoa.)
```
              |D                |Em7              |
```
You've just got to turn it up loud when the flames get higher.
```
|C            |G            |
```
(Oh, whoa, oh, whoa.)
```
              |D            |N.C.            ‖
```
Sing it for the people like us, the people like us.

My Life Would Suck Without You

Words and Music by Lukasz Gottwald,
Max Martin and Claude Kelly

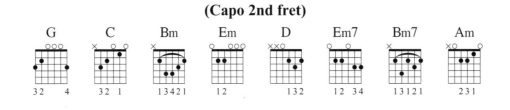

(Capo 2nd fret)

Intro

```
‖G        |       |C      |G      |
|Bm   |Em     |C    |D    |
```

Verse 1

```
‖G                          |        |C      |G      |
   Guess this means you're sor - ry, you're standing at my door.
|Bm                  |Em   |C          |D    |
   Guess this means you take ___ back all you said before,
|G                |C      |
   Like how much you want - ed anyone but me.
|G     |Bm            |Em   |
      You said you'd never come ___ back,
|C          |D    |
But here you are again.
```

Chorus 1

```
|   N.C.            ‖G    |Em7    |C      |
   'Cause we belong ___ togeth - er now, ___ yeah,
|D          |G    |Em7        |Bm7    |
   Forever unit - ed here ___ somehow, ___ yeah.
|D              |G    |Em7   |
   You got a piece ___ of me.
|Am        |C          |
And honestly, ___ my life
|G       |Em7      |C    |D    |
   Would suck ___ without ___ you.
```

Verse 2

```
‖G                    |         |C                   |G         |
    Maybe I was stu - pid for telling you goodbye.
|Bm                |Em      |C                  |D
 Maybe I was wrong ___ for tryin' to pick a fight.
 |G                  |                  |C              |G       |
I know that I've got is - sues, but you're pretty messed up, too.
|Bm                  |Em      |C                 |D      |
 Either way I found ___ out I'm nothing without you.
```

Chorus 2

Repeat Chorus 1

Verse 3

```
‖G                  |         |C            |G
      Being with ___ you is so dysfunctional.
 |Bm                 |Em
I really shouldn't miss ___ you,
  |C              |D            |
But I can't let you go, ___ oh, yeah.
```

Interlude

```
‖ G          |           |C        |G          |
|Bm         |Em          |C        |D          |         |
```

Chorus 3

Repeat Chorus 1

Chorus 4

```
|                    ‖ G        |Em7     |C         |
    'Cause we belong ___ togeth - er now, ___ yeah,
|D          |G          |Em7        |Bm7       |
   Forever unit - ed here ___ somehow, ___ yeah.
|D                  |G         |Em7      |
   You got a piece ___ of me.
|Am            |C          |
 And honestly, ___ my life
|G             |Em7        |C      |D     |G      ‖
    Would suck ___ without ___ you.
```

Run Run Run

Words and Music by Ry Cuming,
Joacim Persson and David Jost

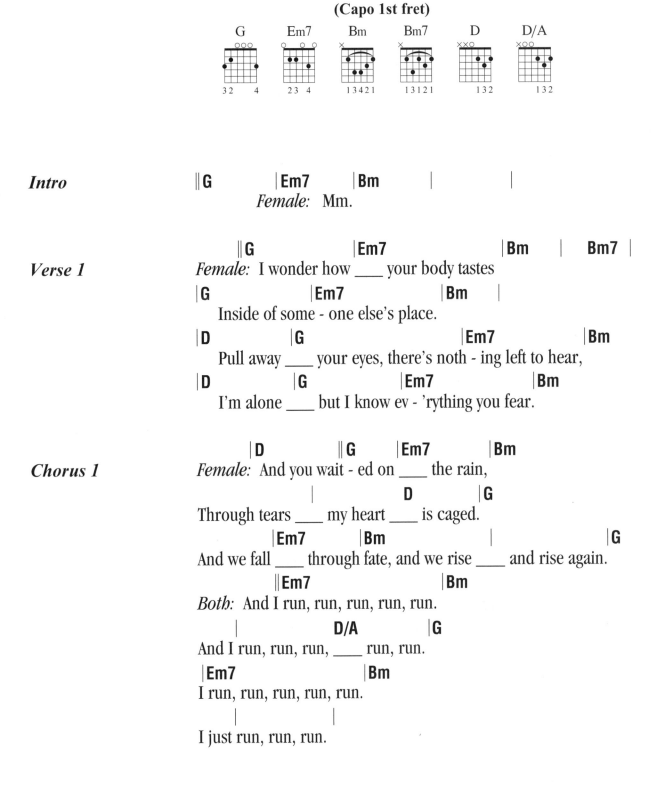

(Capo 1st fret)

Intro

‖G |Em7 |Bm | |

Female: Mm.

Verse 1

‖G |Em7 |Bm | Bm7 |

Female: I wonder how ___ your body tastes

|G |Em7 |Bm |

Inside of some - one else's place.

|D |G |Em7 |Bm

Pull away ___ your eyes, there's noth - ing left to hear,

|D |G |Em7 |Bm

I'm alone ___ but I know ev - 'rything you fear.

Chorus 1

|D   ‖G |Em7 |Bm

Female: And you wait - ed on ___ the rain,

| D |G

Through tears ___ my heart ___ is caged.

|Em7 |Bm | |G

And we fall ___ through fate, and we rise ___ and rise again.

‖Em7 |Bm

Both: And I run, run, run, run, run.

| D/A |G

And I run, run, run, ___ run, run.

|Em7 |Bm

I run, run, run, run, run.

| |

I just run, run, run.

Verse 2

```
‖G                        |Em7        |Bm  |    D  |
```
Male: Tell me how you close ___ the door
```
|G              |Em7                  |Bm    |
```
Knowing nobody ___ can love you more.
```
   |D          |G
```
Both: Telling all ___ your friends
```
          |Em7                    |Bm      |
```
That this love ___ is just made for bleed - ing.
```
|          D            |G
```
Oh, ___ hung up un - derwater
```
        |Em7                      |Bm       |
```
But still ___ we keep on try'n' to breathe ___ in.

Chorus 2

```
|Bm7    D/A           ‖G    |Em7          |Bm
```
Both: And you wait - ed on ___ the rain,
```
              |D/A           |G
```
Male: Through tears ___ my heart is caged.
```
          |Em7        |Bm
```
Both: And we fall ___ through fate,
```
          |D/A                |G
```
Male: And we rise ___ and rise again.
```
      |Em7                  |Bm
```
Both: And I run, run, run, run, run.
```
    |D/A                  |G
```
And I run, run, run, run, run.
```
|Em7              |Bm
```
I run, run, run, run, run.
```
   |              D/A     |
```
I just run, run, run.

Bridge

```
         ‖G  |Em7      |Bm     |        |
```
Female: Our love's for fighting,

```
|G  |Em7 |Bm      |        |
```
Tied up in silence.

Interlude

```
|G          |Em7      |Bm          |     D    |
|G          |Em7      |Bm          |          |
|G          |Em7      |Bm          |     D    |
|G          |Em7      |Bm          |
```

Chorus 3

```
     |D          ‖G     |Em7        |Bm
```
Both: And you wait - ed on ____ the rain,

```
                    |            D          |G
```
Male: Through tears ____ my heart ____ is caged.

```
                 |Em7        |Bm
```
Both: And we fall ____ through fate,

```
                 |              D/A       |
```
Male: And we rise ____ and rise ____ again.

```
‖: G         |Em7                 |Bm
```
Both: And I run, run, run, run, run.

```
     |                  D        :‖ Play 4 times w/ vocal ad lib.
```
And I run, run, run, run, run.

Outro

```
         ‖G  |Em7      |Bm7    |        |
```
Both: Our love's for fighting,

```
|G  |Em7 |Bm      |           ‖
```
Tied up in   silence.

Since U Been Gone

Words and Music by
Max Martin and Lukasz Gottwald

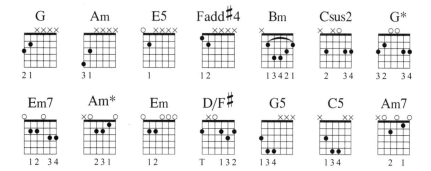

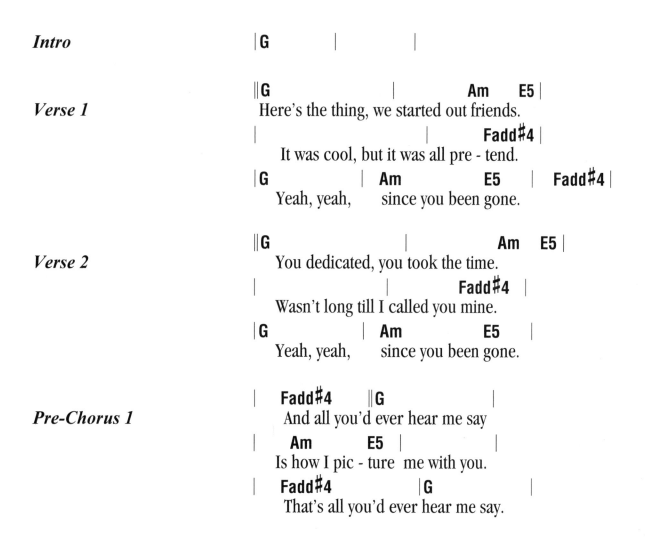

Intro
|G | | |

Verse 1
‖G | Am   E5|
Here's the thing, we started out friends.
| | Fadd#4 |
It was cool, but it was all pre - tend.
|G | Am   E5 | Fadd#4 |
Yeah, yeah,   since you been gone.

Verse 2
‖G | Am   E5|
You dedicated, you took the time.
| | Fadd#4 |
Wasn't long till I called you mine.
|G | Am   E5 | |
Yeah, yeah,   since you been gone.

Pre-Chorus 1
| Fadd#4   ‖G |
And all you'd ever hear me say
| Am   E5 | |
Is how I pic - ture me with you.
| Fadd#4 |G |
That's all you'd ever hear me say.

Chorus 1

```
|         N.C.                ‖Bm    Csus2   G*  |
But since you been gone,
|              |Bm          Csus2  G*   |
I can breathe ___ for the first     time.
|                  |Em7 Csus2  G*   |
I'm so moving on, ____ yeah,    yeah.
|              |Am*          |Em              |D/F♯      |
Thanks to you, ___ now I get ___ what I want,
|Am*                      |G      |        |
Since you been gone.
```

Verse 3

```
‖G                    |              Am    E5  |
How can I put it? You put me on.
|                |        Fadd♯4    |
I even fell for that stupid love song.
|G         |    Am           E5       |
Yeah, yeah,    since you been gone.
```

Pre-Chorus 2

```
|   Fadd♯4        ‖G            |
 How come I never hear you say,
|   Am        E5  |             |
"I just wan - na    be with you?"
|   Fadd♯4        |G            |
Guess you never felt that way.
```

Chorus 2

```
|         N.C.                ‖Bm    Csus2   G*  |
But since you been gone,
|              |Bm          Csus2  G*   |
I can breathe ___ for the first     time.
|                  |Em7 Csus2  G*   |
I'm so moving on, ____ yeah,    yeah.
|                  |Am*          |Em              |D/F♯      |
Thanks to you, ___ now I get, ___  I get what I want,
|Am*                      |
Since you been gone.
```

42

Bridge

```
‖Csus2                    |Em7                    |
   You had your chance, ___ you blew it.
|Csus2        |G5           |
   Out of sight, out of mind.
|C5                         |E5              |
   Shut your mouth, I just ___ can't take it
|C5                    |                    |N.C.(Bm) (C) |(G)        |
   Again and again ___ and again and again.
|(Bm)  (C) |(G)       |(Bm)  (C) |(G)       |
|(Bm)  (C) |
```

Chorus 3

```
|(G)   N.C.                 ‖Bm    Csus2    G* |
     Since you been gone,
|                 |Bm          Csus2  G*   |
   I can breathe ___ for the first     time.
|                       |Em7  Csus2  G*    |
   I'm so moving on, ____ yeah,    yeah.
|                |Am*          |Em
   Thanks to you, ___ now I get,
             |Bm    Csus2   G* |
   I get what I want.
|                 |Bm          Csus2  G*   |
   I can breathe ___ for the first     time.
|                       |Em7  Csus2  G*    |
   I'm so moving on, ____ yeah,    yeah.
|                |Am*          |Em                    |Am*
   Thanks to you, ___ now I get, ___ you should know
        |Em                    |D/F♯  |Am7       |
   That I get, ___ I get what I want,
|                         |G        |            |          |
   Since you been gone, _____     since you been gone,
|                         |        ‖
   Since you been gone.
```

Someone

Words and Music by
Matthew Koma

(Capo 3rd fret)

C   Em7   Am7   F

Intro

‖ C | |Em7 | |

| Am7 | |F | |

Verse 1

‖ C | |Em7 | |

So this is my apology ___ for sayin' all those shitty things

| Am7 | |

I wish I didn't really mean.

| F | |

I'm sorry I'm not sorry.

| C | |

You had your red flags up and raised,

| Em7 | |

More traffic than East L.A,

| Am7 | |F | |

But I drove in anyway, ___ my common sense on holiday.

| C | |

People fall out of phase, we were a crash course.

| Em7 | |Am7 | |

We will just be a place stuck on your passport you travel to sometime.

| |F | |

But I hope you will find

Chorus 1

| ‖ C | |Em7 |

Someone to cry ___ for, ___ someone to try ___ for,

| |Am7 | |F |

Someone to turn ___ your crooked roads ___ into her streets.

| |C | |Em7 |

Someone to fight ___ for, ___ someone to die ___ for,

| |Am7 | |

Someone whose arms ___ will hold you tight ___ enough to be

| F | |C | |

The reason you breathe,

| Em7 | |Am7 | |F | |

Be the reason you breathe.

Verse 2

```
‖C                |                |
    You stay in love like vacation homes.
|Em7             |                      |
    You're like summers on the sunny coast.
|Am7             |                      |
    But when the cold needs a winter coat,
|F               |                      |
    You say you will until you don't.
|C               |                      |
    You wore a compass around your neck,
|Em7             |                      |
    A diff'rent north than we ever read.
|Am7            |                       |
    Well, did you get where you're goin' yet?
|F              |                       |
    Wish you the worst, wish you the best.
|C              |                       |
  I don't know how I fell into your rearview,
|Em7            |
  Paralyzed, lullaby,    I couldn't hear you.
  |Am7                    |    |F          |
So I hope you were right ___ and next to you tonight
```

Chorus 2

```
    |                       ‖C      |           |Em7    |
      There's someone to cry ___ for, ___ someone to try ___ for,
    |              |Am7              |                  |F   |
    Someone to turn ___ your crooked roads ___ into her streets.
    |              |C     |          |Em7    |
    Someone to fight ___ for, ___ someone to die ___ for,
    |              |Am7            |           |
    Someone whose arms ___ will hold you tight ___ enough to be
|F     |           |C     |     |
    The reason you breathe,
|Em7    |          |Am7    |    |F    |    |
    Be the reason you breathe.
```

Outro

```
‖C          |       |Em7       |              |
    So this is my apology ___ for sayin' all those shitty things
|Am7        |              |
    I wish I didn't really mean.
|F        |          |      ‖
    Sorry I'm not sorry.
```

Stronger
(What Doesn't Kill You)

Words and Music by
Greg Kurstin, Jorgen Elofsson, David Gamson
and Alexandra Tamposi

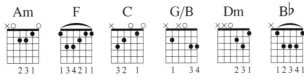

Intro   Am |F |C |G/B ||

Verse 1

Am |F |
    You know the bed feels warm - er

C |G/B |
Sleeping here alone.

Am |F
    You know I dream in col - or

 |C |G/B |
And do the things I want.

Am |
    You think you got the best of me,

F |
Think you've had the last laugh.

C |G/B |
    Bet you think that everything good is gone,

Am |
    Think you left me broken down,

F |
Think that I'd come running back.

C
    Baby, you don't know me,

    |G/B |
'Cause you're dead wrong.

Chorus

N.C.   **Am**
What doesn't kill you makes you stronger,

        F
Stand a little taller.

          C
Doesn't mean I'm lonely when I'm alone.

G/B   **Am**
What doesn't kill you makes a fighter,

        F
Footsteps even lighter.

         C
Doesn't mean I'm over 'cause you're gone.

G/B
What doesn't kill you makes you

Am   **F**
Stronger, strong - er,

   C
Just me, myself, and I.

G/B   **Am**
What doesn't kill you makes you stronger,

        F
Stand a little taller.

         C   **G/B**
Doesn't mean I'm lonely when I'm alone.

Verse 2

Am   **F**   **C**   **G/B**
You heard that I was start - ing over with someone new.

Am   **F**   **C**   **G/B**
They told you I was mov - ing on over you.

Am
You didn't think that I'd come back,

F
I'd come back swinging.

C   **N.C.**
You tried to break me, but you see…

47

Repeat Chorus

Bridge

Dm

Thanks to you I got a new thing started.

B♭

Thanks to you I'm not the brokenhearted.

Am

Thanks to you I'm finally thinking 'bout me.

|F

You know, in the end the day you left

|Am

Was just my begin - ning.

F |C |N.C.

In the end.

Repeat Chorus

Outro

G/B

What doesn't kill you makes you

Am |F

Stronger, strong - er,

|C

Just me, myself, and I.

G/B |Am

What doesn't kill you makes you stronger,

|F

Stand a little taller.

|C |G/B

Doesn't mean I'm lonely when I'm alone,

|Am |F |C |G/B

When I'm alone.

48

Walk Away

Words and Music by
Kelly Clarkson, Chantal Kreviazuk,
Raine Maida and Kara DioGuardi

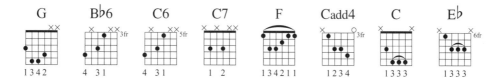

Intro
|| G | B♭6 | C6 | C7 |

Verse 1

|| G | B♭6
        You've got your mother and your brother,

|C6
Ev'ry other under - cover telling you what to say.

|C7   G |B♭6
       You think I'm stupid, but the truth is that it's Cupid, baby;

|C6 |C7
  Loving you has made me this way.

      |G |B♭6
So be - fore you point your fin - ger,

        |C6 |C7
Get your hands ___ off of my trig - ger, oh yeah.

|G |B♭6
      You need to know the situ - ation's getting old,

       |C6 |C7
And now the more you talk, the less I can take.

Chorus 1

```
   ‖G                              |F
```
I'm looking for attention, not ____ another question,
```
      |Cadd4                        |
```
Should ____ you stay or should you go?
```
   |         |G
```
Well, if you don't have the answer,
```
      |F                           |
```
Why ____ you still standing here?
```
|Cadd4              |              |G              |F         |
```
Hey, hey, hey, hey, ____ just walk away.   (Just walk away.
```
|Cadd4         |       |
```
Just walk away.)

Verse 2

```
   ‖G                         |B♭6
```
I've waited here for you like a kid waiting after school,
```
   |C6                              |
```
So tell me how come you never showed?
```
|C7     |G                    |B♭6
```
I gave you ev'rything and never asked for anything,
```
   |C6                  |C7
```
And look at me, I'm all alone.
```
        |G              |B♭6
```
So be - fore you start defend - ing, baby,
```
      |C6                |C7        |
```
Stop ____ all your pretend - ing.
```
|G                         |B♭6
```
I know you know I know, so what's the point in being slow;
```
   |C6                       |C7
```
Let's get this show on the road today.

Chorus 2

Repeat Chorus 1

Bridge

```
‖G                              |
    I want a love, I want a fire,
|Bb6                            |
    To feel the burn, my desires.
|C                              |
    I want a man by my side,
|Eb                             |
    Not a boy runs and hides.
|G                              |
    Are you gonna fight for me,
|Bb6                            |
 Die for me, live and breathe for me?
|C                    |Eb       |
    Do you care for me, 'cause if you don't then just believe
```

Chorus 3

```
    ‖ G                    |F       |
I'm looking for attention, not ___ another question,
        |Cadd4                     |
Should ___ you stay or should you go?
|         |G      |
    Well, if you don't have the answer,
        |F                          |
Why ___ you still standing here?
|Cadd4              |
    Hey, hey, hey, hey, ___ just walk away.
|G                    |F   |Cadd4   |        |
If you don't have the answer, ___      walk away.
|G                        |
         Spoken: Then just leave!
|F              |Cadd4  |
    Walk away.
|        |G    |Bb6   |C6    |C7        |G  N.C.  ‖
Walk away. ___                    Walk away.
```

Underneath the Tree

Words and Music by
Kelly Clarkson and Greg Kurstin

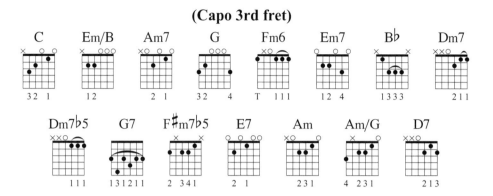

(Capo 3rd fret)

Intro |C Em/B |Am7 G |Fm6 |G |

Chorus 1

‖C | |
You're here, where you should be.

|Em7 |
Snow is falling as the carolers sing.

|B♭ | |Dm7 |Dm7♭5 G7 |
It just wasn't the same, ___ a - lone on Christmas Day.

|C | |
Presents, what a beautiful sight.

|Em7 | |
Don't mean a thing if you ain't holding me tight.

|B♭ | |Dm7 |Dm7♭5 G7 |
You're all that I need _____ underneath the tree.

Verse 1

‖C | |Em7 | |
Tonight ___ I'm gonna hold ___ you close,

|Dm7 | |
Make sure that you know

|Dm7♭5 |G7 |C |
I was lost before ___ you.

| |Em7 |
Christmas was cold ___ and gray,

| |Dm7 | |Dm7♭5 |G7
An - other holiday ___ a - lone to celebrate.

Pre-Chorus 1

```
       ‖F♯m7♭5       |Fm6   |C     E7          |Am
But then ___ one day ___      ev'ry - thing changed.
Am/G              |D7   |G7                    |
You're all I need ___ un - derneath the tree.
```

Chorus 2   *Repeat Chorus 1*

Verse 2

```
       ‖C    |             |Em7    |
I found ___      what I was look - ing for;
 |Dm7                    |
A love that's meant for me,
 |Dm7♭5                  |G7  |C    |
A heart that's mine complete    -    ly.
 |                     |Em7        |
    Knocked me right off ___ my feet,
 |       |Dm7         |       |Dm7♭5      |G7
    And this year I will fall ___ with no worries at all,
```

Pre-Chorus 2

```
       ‖F♯m7♭5       |Fm6   |C     E7          |Am
'Cause you ___ are near ___ and ev'ry - thing's clear.
Am/G              |D7   |G7                    |
You're all I need ___ un - derneath the tree.
```

Chorus 3   *Repeat Chorus 1*

Sax Solo   *Repeat Chorus 1 (Instrumental)*

Pre-Chorus 3

```
       ‖F♯m7♭5       |Fm6   |C     E7          |Am
And then ___ one day ___      ev'ry - thing changed.
Am/G              |D7   |G7                    |
You're all I need ___ un - derneath the tree.
```

Chorus 4   *Repeat Chorus 1*

Outro-Chorus   *Repeat Chorus 1 and fade w/ vocal ad lib.*

STRUM & SING

Lyrics, chord symbols, and guitar chord diagrams for your favorite songs.

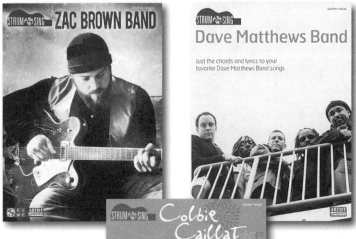

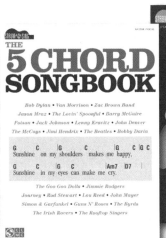

GUITAR

SARA BAREILLES
00102354...$12.99

ZAC BROWN BAND
02501620...$12.99

COLBIE CAILLAT
02501725...$14.99

CAMPFIRE FOLK SONGS
02500686...$10.99

CHART HITS OF 2014-2015
00142554...$12.99

BEST OF KENNY CHESNEY
00142457...$14.99

JOHN DENVER COLLECTION
02500632...$9.95

EASY ACOUSTIC SONGS
00125478...$12.99

50 CHILDREN'S SONGS
02500825...$7.95

THE 5 CHORD SONGBOOK
02501718...$10.99

FOLK SONGS
02501482...$9.99

FOLK/ROCK FAVORITES
02501669...$9.99

40 POP/ROCK HITS
02500633...$9.95

THE 4 CHORD SONGBOOK
02501533...$10.99

THE 4-CHORD COUNTRY SONGBOOK
00114936...$12.99

HITS OF THE '60S
02501138...$10.95

HITS OF THE '70S
02500871...$9.99

HYMNS
02501125...$8.99

JACK JOHNSON
02500858...$16.99

CAROLE KING
00115243...$10.99

DAVE MATTHEWS BAND
02501078...$10.95

JOHN MAYER
02501636...$10.99

INGRID MICHAELSON
02501634...$10.99

THE MOST REQUESTED SONGS
02501748...$10.99

JASON MRAZ
02501452...$14.99

PRAISE & WORSHIP
00152381...$12.99

ROCK AROUND THE CLOCK
00103625...$12.99

ROCK BALLADS
02500872...$9.95

ED SHEERAN
00152016...$12.99

THE 6 CHORD SONGBOOK
02502277...$10.99

CAT STEVENS
00116827...$10.99

TODAY'S HITS
00119301...$10.99

KEITH URBAN
00118558...$12.99

NEIL YOUNG – GREATEST HITS
00138270...$12.99

UKULELE

COLBIE CAILLAT
02501731...$10.99

JOHN DENVER
02501694...$10.99

JACK JOHNSON
02501702...$15.99

JOHN MAYER
02501706...$10.99

INGRID MICHAELSON
02501741...$10.99

THE MOST REQUESTED SONGS
02501453...$14.99

JASON MRAZ
02501753...$14.99

SING-ALONG SONGS
02501710...$14.99

7777 W. BLUEMOUND RD. P.O. BOX 13819 MILWAUKEE, WI 53213

Prices, content, and availability subject to change without notice.

Guitar Chord Songbooks

Each 6" x 9" book includes complete lyrics, chord symbols, and guitar chord diagrams.

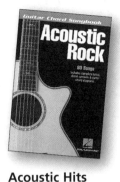

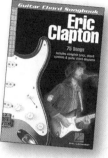
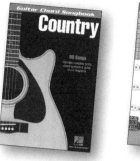
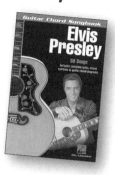

Acoustic Hits
00701787 . . . . $14.99

Acoustic Rock
00699540 . . . . $17.95

Adele
00102761 . . . . $14.99

Alabama
00699914 . . . . $14.95

The Beach Boys
00699566 . . . . $14.95

The Beatles (A-I)
00699558 . . . . $17.99

The Beatles (J-Y)
00699562 . . . . $17.99

Bluegrass
00702585 . . . . $14.99

Blues
00699733 . . . . $12.95

Broadway
00699920 . . . . $14.99

Johnny Cash
00699648 . . . . $17.99

Steven Curtis Chapman
00700702 . . . . $17.99

Children's Songs
00699539 . . . . $16.99

Christmas Carols
00699536 . . . . $12.99

Christmas Songs – 2nd Edition
00119911 . . . . $14.99

Eric Clapton
00699567 . . . . $15.99

Classic Rock
00699598 . . . . $15.99

Coffeehouse Hits
00703318 . . . . $14.99

Country
00699534 . . . . $14.99

Country Favorites
00700609 . . . . $14.99

Country Hits
00140859 . . . . $14.99

Country Standards
00700608 . . . . $12.95

Cowboy Songs
00699636 . . . . $12.95

Creedence Clearwater Revival
00701786 . . . . $12.99

Crosby, Stills & Nash
00701609 . . . . $12.99

John Denver
02501697 . . . . $14.99

Neil Diamond
00700606 . . . . $14.99

Disney
00701071 . . . . $14.99

The Best of Bob Dylan
14037617 . . . . $17.99

Eagles
00122917 . . . . $16.99

Early Rock
00699916 . . . . $14.99

Folksongs
00699541 . . . . $12.95

Folk Pop Rock
00699651 . . . . $14.95

40 Easy Strumming Songs
00115972 . . . . $14.99

Four Chord Songs
00701611 . . . . $12.99

Glee
00702501 . . . . $14.99

Gospel Hymns
00700463 . . . . $14.99

Grand Ole Opry®
00699885 . . . . $16.95

Green Day
00103074 . . . . $12.99

Guitar Chord Songbook White Pages
00702609 . . . . $29.99

Irish Songs
00701044 . . . . $14.99

Billy Joel
00699632 . . . . $15.99

Elton John
00699732 . . . . $15.99

Ray LaMontagne
00130337 . . . . $12.99

Latin Songs
00700973 . . . . $14.99

Love Songs
00701043 . . . . $14.99

Bob Marley
00701704 . . . . $12.99

Bruno Mars
00125332 . . . . $12.99

Paul McCartney
00385035 . . . . $16.95

Steve Miller
00701146 . . . . $12.99

Modern Worship
00701801 . . . . $16.99

Motown
00699734 . . . . $16.95

The 1950s
00699922 . . . . $14.99

The 1980s
00700551 . . . . $16.99

Nirvana
00699762 . . . . $16.99

Roy Orbison
00699752 . . . . $12.95

Peter, Paul & Mary
00103013 . . . . $12.99

Tom Petty
00699883 . . . . $15.99

Pop/Rock
00699538 . . . . $14.95

Praise & Worship
00699634 . . . . $14.99

Elvis Presley
00699633 . . . . $14.95

Queen
00702395 . . . . $12.99

Rascal Flatts
00130951 . . . . $12.99

Red Hot Chili Peppers
00699710 . . . . $16.95

Rock Ballads
00701034 . . . . $14.99

Rock 'n' Roll
00699535 . . . . $14.95

Bob Seger
00701147 . . . . $12.99

Carly Simon
00121011 . . . . $14.99

Singer/Songwriter Songs
00126053 . . . . $14.99

Sting
00699921 . . . . $14.99

Taylor Swift
00701799 . . . . $15.99

Three Chord Acoustic Songs
00123860 . . . . $14.99

Three Chord Songs
00699720 . . . . $12.95

Today's Hits
00120983 . . . . $14.99

Top 100 Hymns Guitar Songbook
75718017 . . . . $14.99

Two-Chord Songs
00119236 . . . . $14.99

Ultimate-Guitar
00702617 . . . . $24.99

U2
00137744 . . . . $14.99

Wedding Songs
00701005 . . . . $14.99

Hank Williams
00700607 . . . . $14.99

Stevie Wonder
00120862 . . . . $14.99

Neil Young–Decade
00700464 . . . . $14.99

Prices, contents, and availability subject to change without notice.

HAL•LEONARD®
CORPORATION

7777 W. BLUEMOUND RD. P.O. BOX 13819 MILWAUKEE, WI 53213

Visit Hal Leonard online at **www.halleonard.com**

0915

HAL•LEONARD GUITAR PLAY-ALONG

This series will help you play your favorite songs quickly and easily. Just follow the tab and listen to the audio to the hear how the guitar should sound, and then play along using the separate backing tracks. Mac or PC users can also slow down the tempo without changing pitch by using the CD in their computer. The melody and lyrics are included in the book so that you can sing or simply follow along.

INCLUDES TAB

VOL. 1 – ROCK	00699570 / $16.99	
VOL. 2 – ACOUSTIC	00699569 / $16.95	
VOL. 3 – HARD ROCK	00699573 / $16.95	
VOL. 4 – POP/ROCK	00699571 / $16.99	
VOL. 5 – MODERN ROCK	00699574 / $16.99	
VOL. 6 – '90S ROCK	00699572 / $16.99	
VOL. 7 – BLUES	00699575 / $16.95	
VOL. 8 – ROCK	00699585 / $14.99	
VOL. 10 – ACOUSTIC	00699586 / $16.95	
VOL. 11 – EARLY ROCK	00699579 / $14.95	
VOL. 12 – POP/ROCK	00699587 / $14.95	
VOL. 13 – FOLK ROCK	00699581 / $15.99	
VOL. 14 – BLUES ROCK	00699582 / $16.95	
VOL. 15 – R&B	00699583 / $14.95	
VOL. 16 – JAZZ	00699584 / $15.95	
VOL. 17 – COUNTRY	00699588 / $15.95	
VOL. 18 – ACOUSTIC ROCK	00699577 / $15.95	
VOL. 19 – SOUL	00699578 / $14.99	
VOL. 20 – ROCKABILLY	00699580 / $14.95	
VOL. 21 – YULETIDE	00699602 / $14.95	
VOL. 22 – CHRISTMAS	00699600 / $15.95	
VOL. 23 – SURF	00699635 / $14.95	
VOL. 24 – ERIC CLAPTON	00699649 / $17.99	
VOL. 25 – LENNON & MCCARTNEY	00699642 / $16.99	
VOL. 26 – ELVIS PRESLEY	00699643 / $14.95	
VOL. 27 – DAVID LEE ROTH	00699645 / $16.95	
VOL. 28 – GREG KOCH	00699646 / $14.95	
VOL. 29 – BOB SEGER	00699647 / $15.99	
VOL. 30 – KISS	00699644 / $16.99	
VOL. 31 – CHRISTMAS HITS	00699652 / $14.95	
VOL. 32 – THE OFFSPRING	00699653 / $14.95	
VOL. 33 – ACOUSTIC CLASSICS	00699656 / $16.95	
VOL. 34 – CLASSIC ROCK	00699658 / $16.95	
VOL. 35 – HAIR METAL	00699660 / $16.95	
VOL. 36 – SOUTHERN ROCK	00699661 / $16.95	
VOL. 37 – ACOUSTIC UNPLUGGED	00699662 / $22.99	
VOL. 38 – BLUES	00699663 / $16.95	
VOL. 39 – '80S METAL	00699664 / $16.99	
VOL. 40 – INCUBUS	00699668 / $17.95	
VOL. 41 – ERIC CLAPTON	00699669 / $16.95	
VOL. 42 – 2000S ROCK	00699670 / $16.99	
VOL. 43 – LYNYRD SKYNYRD	00699681 / $17.95	
VOL. 44 – JAZZ	00699689 / $14.99	
VOL. 45 – TV THEMES	00699718 / $14.95	
VOL. 46 – MAINSTREAM ROCK	00699722 / $16.95	
VOL. 47 – HENDRIX SMASH HITS	00699723 / $19.95	
VOL. 48 – AEROSMITH CLASSICS	00699724 / $17.99	
VOL. 49 – STEVIE RAY VAUGHAN	00699725 / $17.99	
VOL. 50 – VAN HALEN 1978-1984	00110269 / $17.99	
VOL. 51 – ALTERNATIVE '90S	00699727 / $14.99	
VOL. 52 – FUNK	00699728 / $14.95	
VOL. 53 – DISCO	00699729 / $14.99	
VOL. 54 – HEAVY METAL	00699730 / $14.95	
VOL. 55 – POP METAL	00699731 / $14.95	
VOL. 56 – FOO FIGHTERS	00699749 / $15.99	
VOL. 57 – SYSTEM OF A DOWN	00699751 / $14.95	
VOL. 58 – BLINK-182	00699772 / $14.95	
VOL. 59 – CHET ATKINS	00702347 / $16.99	
VOL. 60 – 3 DOORS DOWN	00699774 / $14.95	
VOL. 61 – SLIPKNOT	00699775 / $16.99	
VOL. 62 – CHRISTMAS CAROLS	00699798 / $12.95	

VOL. 63 – CREEDENCE CLEARWATER REVIVAL	00699802 / $16.99	
VOL. 64 – THE ULTIMATE OZZY OSBOURNE	00699803 / $16.99	
VOL. 66 – THE ROLLING STONES	00699807 / $16.95	
VOL. 67 – BLACK SABBATH	00699808 / $16.99	
VOL. 68 – PINK FLOYD – DARK SIDE OF THE MOON	00699809 / $16.99	
VOL. 69 – ACOUSTIC FAVORITES	00699810 / $14.95	
VOL. 70 – OZZY OSBOURNE	00699805 / $16.99	
VOL. 71 – CHRISTIAN ROCK	00699824 / $14.95	
VOL. 73 – BLUESY ROCK	00699829 / $16.99	
VOL. 75 – TOM PETTY	00699882 / $16.99	
VOL. 76 – COUNTRY HITS	00699884 / $14.95	
VOL. 77 – BLUEGRASS	00699910 / $14.99	
VOL. 78 – NIRVANA	00700132 / $16.99	
VOL. 79 – NEIL YOUNG	00700133 / $24.99	
VOL. 80 – ACOUSTIC ANTHOLOGY	00700175 / $19.95	
VOL. 81 – ROCK ANTHOLOGY	00700176 / $22.99	
VOL. 82 – EASY SONGS	00700177 / $12.99	
VOL. 83 – THREE CHORD SONGS	00700178 / $16.99	
VOL. 84 – STEELY DAN	00700200 / $16.99	
VOL. 85 – THE POLICE	00700269 / $16.99	
VOL. 86 – BOSTON	00700465 / $16.99	
VOL. 87 – ACOUSTIC WOMEN	00700763 / $14.99	
VOL. 88 – GRUNGE	00700467 / $16.99	
VOL. 89 – REGGAE	00700468 / $15.99	
VOL. 90 – CLASSICAL POP	00700469 / $14.99	
VOL. 91 – BLUES INSTRUMENTALS	00700505 / $14.99	
VOL. 92 – EARLY ROCK INSTRUMENTALS	00700506 / $14.99	
VOL. 93 – ROCK INSTRUMENTALS	00700507 / $16.99	
VOL. 94 – SLOW BLUES	00700508 / $16.99	
VOL. 95 – BLUES CLASSICS	00700509 / $14.99	
VOL. 96 – THIRD DAY	00700560 / $14.95	
VOL. 97 – ROCK BAND	00700703 / $14.99	
VOL. 99 – ZZ TOP	00700762 / $16.99	
VOL. 100 – B.B. KING	00700466 / $16.99	
VOL. 101 – SONGS FOR BEGINNERS	00701917 / $14.99	
VOL. 102 – CLASSIC PUNK	00700769 / $14.99	
VOL. 103 – SWITCHFOOT	00700773 / $16.99	
VOL. 104 – DUANE ALLMAN	00700846 / $16.99	
VOL. 105 – LATIN	00700939 / $16.99	
VOL. 106 – WEEZER	00700958 / $14.99	
VOL. 107 – CREAM	00701069 / $16.99	
VOL. 108 – THE WHO	00701053 / $16.99	
VOL. 109 – STEVE MILLER	00701054 / $14.99	
VOL. 110 – SLIDE GUITAR HITS	00701055 / $16.99	
VOL. 111 – JOHN MELLENCAMP	00701056 / $14.99	
VOL. 112 – QUEEN	00701052 / $16.99	
VOL. 113 – JIM CROCE	00701058 / $15.99	
VOL. 114 – BON JOVI	00701060 / $14.99	
VOL. 115 – JOHNNY CASH	00701070 / $16.99	
VOL. 116 – THE VENTURES	00701124 / $14.99	
VOL. 117 – BRAD PAISLEY	00701224 / $16.99	
VOL. 118 – ERIC JOHNSON	00701353 / $16.99	
VOL. 119 – AC/DC CLASSICS	00701356 / $17.99	
VOL. 120 – PROGRESSIVE ROCK	00701457 / $14.99	
VOL. 121 – U2	00701508 / $16.99	
VOL. 122 – CROSBY, STILLS & NASH	00701610 / $16.99	
VOL. 123 – LENNON & MCCARTNEY ACOUSTIC	00701614 / $16.99	
VOL. 124 – MODERN WORSHIP	00701629 / $14.99	

VOL. 125 – JEFF BECK	00701687 / $16.99	
VOL. 126 – BOB MARLEY	00701701 / $16.99	
VOL. 127 – 1970S ROCK	00701739 / $14.99	
VOL. 128 – 1960S ROCK	00701740 / $14.99	
VOL. 129 – MEGADETH	00701741 / $16.99	
VOL. 131 – 1990S ROCK	00701743 / $14.99	
VOL. 132 – COUNTRY ROCK	00701757 / $15.99	
VOL. 133 – TAYLOR SWIFT	00701894 / $16.99	
VOL. 134 – AVENGED SEVENFOLD	00701906 / $16.99	
VOL. 136 – GUITAR THEMES	00701922 / $14.99	
VOL. 137 – IRISH TUNES	00701966 / $15.99	
VOL. 138 – BLUEGRASS CLASSICS	00701967 / $14.99	
VOL. 139 – GARY MOORE	00702370 / $16.99	
VOL. 140 – MORE STEVIE RAY VAUGHAN	00702396 / $17.99	
VOL. 141 – ACOUSTIC HITS	00702401 / $16.99	
VOL. 144 – DJANGO REINHARDT	00702531 / $16.99	
VOL. 145 – DEF LEPPARD	00702532 / $16.99	
VOL. 146 – ROBERT JOHNSON	00702533 / $16.99	
VOL. 147 – SIMON & GARFUNKEL	14041591 / $16.99	
VOL. 148 – BOB DYLAN	14041592 / $16.99	
VOL. 149 – AC/DC HITS	14041593 / $17.99	
VOL. 150 – ZAKK WYLDE	02501717 / $16.99	
VOL. 152 – JOE BONAMASSA	02501751 / $19.99	
VOL. 153 – RED HOT CHILI PEPPERS	00702990 / $19.99	
VOL. 155 – ERIC CLAPTON – FROM THE ALBUM UNPLUGGED	00703085 / $16.99	
VOL. 156 – SLAYER	00703770 / $17.99	
VOL. 157 – FLEETWOOD MAC	00101382 / $16.99	
VOL. 158 – ULTIMATE CHRISTMAS	00101889 / $14.99	
VOL. 160 – T-BONE WALKER	00102641 / $16.99	
VOL. 161 – THE EAGLES – ACOUSTIC	00102659 / $17.99	
VOL. 162 – THE EAGLES HITS	00102667 / $17.99	
VOL. 163 – PANTERA	00103036 / $17.99	
VOL. 164 – VAN HALEN 1986-1995	00110270 / $17.99	
VOL. 166 – MODERN BLUES	00700764 / $16.99	
VOL. 168 – KISS	00113421 / $16.99	
VOL. 169 – TAYLOR SWIFT	00115982 / $16.99	
VOL. 170 – THREE DAYS GRACE	00117337 / $16.99	
VOL. 171 – JAMES BROWN	00117420 / $16.99	
VOL. 172 – THE DOOBIE BROTHERS	00119670 / $16.99	
VOL. 174 – SCORPIONS	00122119 / $16.99	
VOL. 175 – MICHAEL SCHENKER	00122127 / $16.99	
VOL. 176 – BLUES BREAKERS WITH JOHN MAYALL & ERIC CLAPTON	00122132 / $19.99	
VOL. 177 – ALBERT KING	00123271 / $16.99	
VOL. 178 – JASON MRAZ	00124165 / $17.99	
VOL. 179 – RAMONES	00127073 / $16.99	
VOL. 180 – BRUNO MARS	00129706 / $16.99	
VOL. 181 – JACK JOHNSON	00129854 / $16.99	
VOL. 182 – SOUNDGARDEN	00138161 / $17.99	
VOL. 184 – KENNY WAYNE SHEPHERD	00138258 / $17.99	

Complete song lists available online.

Prices, contents, and availability subject to change without notice.

HAL•LEONARD® CORPORATION

7777 W. BLUEMOUND RD. P.O. BOX 13819 MILWAUKEE, WI 53213

www.halleonard.com

0815